Meditations for Addictive Behavior

A System of Yogic Science with Nutritional Formulas

I WAS THERE PRESS

ISBN-13 978-0-9799192-1-3
ISBN-10 0-9799192-1-5

Layout and Design by Kendra Mack www.kendramack.net

All images © 2007, Todd Hollien except pages 14, 20, 24, 28, 32, 36, 40, 44, 50, 54, 58. 62, 66, 68 and 70 © 2007, Kendra Mack.

Printed in China
By Pettit Network, Inc, Afton, MN
www.pettitnetwork.com

Distributed by Itasca Books
3501 Hwy. 100 South, Suite 220 Minneapolis, MN 55416
800-901-3480 www.itascabooks.com

This publication has received the KRI Seal of Approval. This Seal is given only to products that have been reviewed for accuracy and integrity of the sections containing the 3HO lifestyle and Kundalini Yoga as taught by Yogi Bhajan.

Meditations for Addictive Behavior

A System of Yogic Science with Nutritional Formulas

The Super Health Way from Recovery to Self-Discovery as taught by Yogi Bhajan

Mukta Kaur Khalsa, Ph.D.

Super Health is an affiliate of the 3HO Foundation.

HOW TO USE THIS BOOK

This book is a guide to change behavior. After reading the beginning sections, it is time for action. You may start with Meditation 1 or you may choose any other meditation that deals with an issue you are currently working on. Since yogic science believes that it takes 40 days to break an addiction or create a new habit, you are encouraged to practice a meditation a day for this amount of time to get its maximum benefit. Making this commitment will work for you.

MEDICAL DISCLAIMER

Please be advised that the information contained in this manual is not a substitute for medical detoxification or treatment. It is an educational program, designed to use the ancient wisdom of humanology* and yoga to support the recovery of a user. As emphasized in all medical substance abuse treatment programs, abstinence is the first step. Combining Kundalini Yoga with alcohol or drug use may be harmful to physical and mental health.

We encourage you to establish abstinence from alcohol and drug use.

Table of Contents

Dedication

This book is dedicated to my beloved teacher, Yogi Bhajan. He came to the West and saw people turning to drugs to fill a hollowness inside. He said, "Drugs are a Drag" and gave a practical technology for everyday living to propel us to our own excellence. As a tireless ambassador he inspired people to elevate the human spirit to have the dignity of self autonomy.

May his teachings be used to exalt the self to a God-conscious reality of happiness, health and prosperity.

May we have the blessing to serve humanity by living through your example of compassion and love.

— Mukta Kaur Khalsa

Mukta Kaur Khalsa, Director of SuperHealth, personally studied the teachings for addictive behavior with Yogi Bhajan from 1973 until his death in 2004. She directed a specialized rehabilitation hospital in Tucson, AZ and more recently ran a pilot program in collaboration with the Punjab government in India. She is co-author of a recently published research paper on the results of the India program. Mukta is the 3HO UN representative to the Office of Drug Control and Crime, Vienna. She currently conducts training workshops around the world on SuperHealth technology.

Foreword

This isn't a complicated book you're holding in your hands. It's reader friendly, with easy to follow directions. Can something this simple be effective? Yes, it can!

From her 35 years of experience working with addiction, Mukta has selected, organized, and beautifully presented twelve special gems out of the treasure chest of yogic technology delivered by the Master of Kundalini Yoga*, Yogi Bhajan.

Most of our lives are spent doing things out of habit — how we walk, talk, dress, eat, and especially how we think! Some habits are beneficial, but many are not. They tear us down and only give us temporary pleasure. Yogi Bhajan called these "self-defeating habits." When they get out of control, they become addictions.

Overcoming our addictions can seem daunting. The key to change is to substitute positive habits for self-defeating ones. "Meditations for Addictive Behavior" is full of positive habits you can incorporate into your daily life to replace the addictive ones that are jeopardizing your health and happiness. It is your birthright as a human being to be healthy and happy. Claim it!

By practicing these twelve meditations, utilizing the nutritional tips, and reading Yogi Bhajan's inspiring words — words that speak directly to your soul — you can accelerate your self-healing process and enhance your personal spiritual awareness.

So take the first step. Try the first meditation. Make it a habit and see for yourself: "Doing is believing."

I am grateful to Mukta for giving us a book which is truly a treasure and a blessing for those who are ready to improve their lives.

— Shakti Parwha Kaur Khalsa

Shakti Parwha Kaur Khalsa was Yogi Bhajan's first student in the United States. She is the author of *Kundalini Yoga: The Flow of Eternal Power* and *Marriage on the Spiritual Path: Mastering the Highest Yoga*.

Introduction

In 1968, Yogi Bhajan came to America to teach Kundalini Yoga. At that time people in the West were seeking spiritual fulfillment. He found the youth using drugs to escape the emptiness and isolation of their cultural environment. Middle class housewives were taking pills with the distorted hope it would numb them from an inner unhappiness. Businessmen used alcohol to deal with the stress of everyday living.

Yogi Bhajan addressed these problems at a grassroots level. He started teaching Kundalini Yoga and meditation classes, and slowly people discovered a way of feeling good naturally. As an experiment, he housed two heroin addicts in his center in Washington, D.C. For two weeks, in a 24/7 controlled environment, he implemented a treatment program based on Kundalini Yoga and meditation. An amazing thing happened. They overcame their addiction and were changed men. This was the birth of SuperHealth.

Inspired by the results in Washington, the Tucson, Arizona center treated its first substance abuser. This was the beginning of a residential program. In 1978 SuperHealth became accredited by the prestigious Joint Commission on Accreditation of Healthcare Organizations. Later, the Joint Commission rated SuperHealth in the top 10% of all treatment programs throughout the United States.

SuperHealth developed into a systemized program with customized treatment plans for behavioral addictions including stress, substance abuse and other unhealthy habits and emotional disorders. The program included three Kundalini Yoga and meditation classes each day; a specific detoxification and rehabilitation diet complete with fresh juices; a vitamin and herbal regime; therapeutic massages; Humanology* sessions, and individual, family and spiritual counseling.

In 2004 Yogi Bhajan's promise that his teachings would be brought back to India became a reality. In collaboration with the Punjab government, SuperHealth was invited to conduct a 90-day pilot project for drug users in Amritsar, India. The program opened in October of that year with a volunteer team of professionals. This experience profoundly changed lives. A research paper on the effectiveness of the program in Amritsar was published in "The Journal of Ethnicity and Substance Abuse" in 2008.

Problems of addictive behaviors and unhealthy habits and lifestyles are rampant. To address this concern, SuperHealth is conducting training programs for yoga teachers and healthcare professionals. Once trained, these people will be able to serve their local communities.

We offer "Meditations for Addictive Behavior" with inspirational words, simple meditations and nutritional tips for you to use in your everyday life.

It is our blessing to share these teachings with you. The experience is more easily understood by the heart than by the mind.

Yogi Bhajan taught that the birthright of all people is to be happy and live in peace. This is our prayer.

Yogi Bhajan (1929-2004)

Millions of people around the world know of Yogi Bhajan. He was a dynamic teacher and master of Kundalini Yoga.

In 1968 he left India to bring to America the yogic and meditative technology of Kundalini Yoga, which he mastered at an early age. He founded the "3HO* Foundation," the Healthy, Happy, Holy Organization, a non-profit dedicated to the physical, mental and spiritual well-being of the individual.

Today, the 3HO Foundation operates throughout the world with 300 centers in 35 countries. Over 200 books and videos have been produced on Kundalini Yoga and meditation

In 1973 SuperHealth opened its doors and began blending the ancient formulas of the East with the innovations of the West. These precious and sacred teachings revolutionized the therapeutic model for behavioral addiction.

Yogi Bhajan's inspiration and guidance helped create industries as diverse as health food manufacturing (Yogi Tea and Peace Cereal) and security services (Akal Security).

He is one of four humanitarians to have received a Joint Congressional Resolution by the United States Congress honoring his life's work and teachings. The other recipients were Mother Teresa, Martin Luther King and Pope John Paul II.

Yogi Bhajan passed away October 6, 2004.

Kundalini Yoga

Kundalini Yoga is known as the "Yoga of Awareness." Its practice rebuilds and strengthens the nervous system which is directly affected by substance abuse and other addictions. Yogi Bhajan said, "Kundalini Yoga gives a person back their own strength, it gives them discipline, changes the chemistry of the blood, stimulates the glandular system and also teaches a person to relax." Meditation promotes clarity of thought and Kundalini Yoga provides the discipline to carry it out. Through this technology the addictive personality is given immunity to protect itself from the pressures of society.

Breathing

Conscious breathing is an important part of living. Increased breath capacity developed through long deep breathing exercises carries more oxygen to the brain, which in turn helps to create a heightened sense of awareness.

Science has shown that conscious controlled breathing can also elevate your mood, create relaxation and shield you from the effects of stress, aid in pain control, and alleviate a wide range of symptoms like headaches or indigestion.

The most beneficial way of breathing is to inhale completely, filling your abdomen with the breath. Then bring it slowly up to the lungs, completely expanding them. Exhale slowly and completely. By intentionally focusing attention on your breath, you are practicing conscious breathing.

By changing the rhythm and depth of your breath you can begin to change addictive behavioral patterns.

In today's modern times of behavioral addiction, the sacred science of Kundalini yoga and meditation offers a solution to the pressures of our global society.

Meditation

The practice of meditation provides the psychological edge necessary to remain calm and non-reactive under challenging situations. Additional benefits of meditation are self-discipline, peace of mind, increased self-esteem and a greater awareness or higher consciousness. Beyond these general benefits, each meditation can be used for the specific effects noted in shaded boxes at the end of the meditation. Daily practice creates clarity and self-control helpful in overcoming behavioral addictions.

Before beginning your practice or sharing these teachings with others, tune in with the phrase, "Ong Namo Guru Dev Namo."* (See glossary for simple instructions.) The meaning of these sounds, "I bow to the Creator, the divine teacher within," promotes hope, strength and courage and begins to break old habits and bring change to your life. It is also beneficial, although not required, to cover your head during meditation to conserve and focus the energy.

"Meditation is the art of breaking habits to purify the mind and to take care of day to day affairs"
- Yogi Bhajan

From Recovery to Self-Discovery

In today's world of quick fixes, we strive for ease and comfort. It is easy to slip into complacency and go to sleep in our own lives. In this state, challenges in life tend to take us by surprise. We don't understand how it can happen and ask, "Why me?"

The meditations in this book are tools to enable us to deal with obstacles in life that seem insurmountable. This can be part of our recovery program to awaken self-discovery.

A former substance abuser who completed SuperHealth in 1991 now lives a drug-free life working as a social worker. She says, "This program helped me to reduce urges and gave me the stamina to make the right decisions. The yogic practices I learned helped to eliminate internal dialogue and let me choose what actions, thoughts and words would lead me down the path of sobriety and, thus, enlightenment. The fortitude and strength I gained left little room for personal arguments."

The Meditations and Breathing Techniques

Meditation 1
The Healthy Happy Holy* Breath

- Sit with spine straight in a chair* or cross-legged. Hands are relaxed and resting on the knees.

- Close the eyes and focus them at the point between the eyebrows.

- Take a deep full breath inhaling through the nose. Hold the breath pulling the chest forward.

- Silently repeat the words (mantra*) 3 times: *This takes 15 seconds Total.*
"Healthy am I, Happy am I, Holy am I."

- As you exhale repeat the words out loud 3 times.

Practice for 11 minutes.

- To end, inhale deeply, completely filling the lungs with the breath. Exhale and relax.

- Sit in silence for 1 - 2 minutes.

- Inhale deeply and stretch arms over the head with fingers interlocked while pulling up the spine.

- Exhale and relax.

This is a self-healing mantra. It empowers us and enhances our self-control and our ability to carry out our intentions. We have the right to be happy and at peace with ourselves.

Holy* refers to wholeness. *, the balance of one's physical, mental & spiritual being*

18 W.H.O. defines Human Health "as a state of complete physical, mental and social well being.

Nutritional Tip 1
Water

For cleansing the body of toxins, balancing the emotions and calming the nervous system, sip 2 quarts of water every day.

*An attitude of gratitude
brings you opportunities beyond
your concept.*

- Yogi Bhajan

Meditation 2
Breath for Energy

- Sit with spine straight in a chair or cross-legged. Palms are together at the heart center* in Prayer Pose* with thumbs pressed against the sternum. Focus between the eyebrows, with eyelids slightly closed.

- Inhale through the nose in 4 equal parts (like sniffs.) Hold a few seconds. Exhale in 4 equal parts. On each of the sniffs, powerfully pull in the navel point.*
  Use SAA-TAA-NAA-MAA Mantra to reduce Anxiety/Confusion

Practice for 3 - 5 minutes.

- To end, inhale deeply, and press palms together with maximum force for 10 seconds. Then exhale.

- Relax for 15 - 20 seconds.

- Repeat this sequence 2 more times.

AFTER, can lie on back 2 Min. Relax each body part.
Then 2-3 L.D. breaths, stretch & rise.

This meditation helps to overcome anxiety, confusion and commotions of the mind through conscious breathing. It connects us with our inner selves and allows us to experience a power greater than ourselves. This will positively affect our state of mind! It relieves fatigue, relaxes & energizes

22

Nutritional Tip 2
The Wonders of Grapefruit Juice!

An 8 oz. glass helps in the detoxification process and is also good for the kidneys and urination. Use fresh juices whenever possible.

*Human must learn to accomplish
and to achieve.*

*Happiness comes when you have
the most impossible challenge
and you make it.*

*There is no substitute for victory
and excellence.*

– Yogi Bhajan

Meditation 3
God and Me, Me and God Are One

- Sit with spine straight in a chair or cross-legged. Palms are together at the heart center in Prayer Pose with thumbs pressed at the heart center. Eyes are closed.

- In a monotone, recite:
  "God and me, me and God are one." *Each repeat takes 5 seconds.*

  As God's creation, we are all one. Say it out loud with conviction. Feel it.

Practice for 3 minutes in a monotone.

- To end, inhale, hold the breath a few seconds, then exhale and relax.

This meditation helps affirm that God is within. As God's creation we are all one.

Nutritional Tip 3
Grapefruit, Apple and Carrot Juice

A wonderful detoxification drink. Very cleansing as well as an energy booster.
Combine 1/3 grapefruit juice, 1/3 apple juice, 1/3 carrot juice (8 oz. total).

*Every individual is made in God
and is beyond judgment.*

– Yogi Bhajan

Meditation 4
Stress Relief and Clearing Emotions of the Past

- Sit with spine straight in a chair or cross-legged. Place your hands at the center of your chest, tips of the thumbs and each finger touching the corresponding fingers on the opposite hand. Fingertips are pointing upward. There is space between the palms.

- Look at the tip of your nose* and inhale for 5 seconds. Hold for 5 seconds. Exhale for 5 seconds.

Practice for 11 minutes.

- To end, inhale, hold the breath for a few seconds then exhale and relax.

This meditation is useful for dealing with stress, difficult relationships, past family issues and unresolved emotional conflicts.

Nutritional Tip 4
Celery Juice

To calm and strengthen the nervous system, drink an 8 oz. glass. Or, if celery juice is not available, drink carrot juice.

It's not the life that matters;
it's the courage that you bring to it.

— Yogi Bhajan

Meditation 5
Meditation to Conquer Self-Animosity

- Sit with spine straight in a chair or cross-legged. Apply neck lock.* (Gently move the chin towards the back of the neck, keeping the muscles of the throat and face relaxed.)

- Relax the arms at the sides and raise the forearms up and in, toward the chest at the heart level, with palms facing toward each other.

- Make the hands into fists, pointing the thumbs straight up and pressing the sides of the thumbs and knuckles of the fingers together. Focus the eyes at the tip of the nose.

- Inhale fully through the nose. Exhale completely through the mouth. Inhale through the mouth. Exhale through the nose.

Practice for 3 minutes. Gradually build to 11 minutes. Do not exceed 22 minutes.

- To end, inhale and stretch the arms overhead. Maintain this posture and then exhale. Keep the stretched position as you take 3 more deep breaths. Relax.

Our greatest enemy is our mind. A self-defeating attitude and self-animosity exist when we do not accept ourselves.

This meditation enhances the capacity to confront and experience the self in relationship to God.

Nutritional Tip 5
Bananas

Bananas strengthen the nervous system and are good for depression. Eat 1 - 4 bananas daily. Be sure to scrape the inside of the banana to get all the nutrients.

Praying is talking to God;
meditating is letting God talk to you.

– Yogi Bhajan

Meditation 6
Self Blessing Meditation

- Sit with spine straight in a chair or cross-legged, eyes closed.

- Arch the right arm over the head, palm facing down 6 inches above the crown of the head.

- Raise the left forearm parallel to the ground. Bend the elbow so the hand is touching your chest, palm facing down.

- Repeat out loud in a monotone:
  "I bless myself, I bless myself, I bless myself. I am, I am."

Practice for 3 minutes.

- To end, inhale deeply, hold the breath and repeat the mantra mentally. Exhale.

- Repeat this sequence 2 more times. Relax.

This meditation frees us from guilt, blame, shame, resentment and bitterness. By blessing ourselves, God immediately and spontaneously blesses us.

Nutritional Tip 6
Yogi Tea

Yogi Tea is a blood purifier and energy booster. It is also good for digestion, the nervous system and bones. Prepare fresh ingredients or, for your convenience, go to your local health food store and find pre-made Classic Yogi Tea bags boxed on the shelves.

To prepare use:
10 oz. water
3 whole cloves
4 whole green cardamom pods
4 black peppercorns
1/2 stick cinnamon
1 slice ginger root
1/4 tsp. or 1 small bag of black tea
1 cup of milk

Combine spices and water in a pot and boil for 20 - 30 minutes. Take off the heat and add the black tea, steeping for a couple of minutes. Add milk and bring to a boil. Remove from the heat and strain. Add honey to taste. Makes 1 cup.

Patience pays. Wait.
Let the hand of God work for you.

— Yogi Bhajan

Meditation 7
Meditation for the Negative Mind

- Sit with spine straight in a chair or cross-legged.

- Make a cup of the hands with both palms facing up. The right hand rests on top of the left hand. The right fingers cross over the left fingers.

- Place cup at the heart center. Elbows are relaxed at the sides.

- Eyes are slightly open and look down towards the hands.

- Inhale deeply through the nose. Exhale through rounded lips. You will feel the breath on your hands.

- As you inhale, allow unwanted desires and negative thoughts to enter your mind. As you exhale, completely let them go.

Practice for 11 minutes to begin. Work up to 31 minutes per day.

- To end, inhale powerfully, exhale completely through the nose. Repeat this breath 3 to 5 times. Then relax completely.

This meditation helps to shield us from negativity. It clears the mind of unwanted, negative or fearful thoughts, protecting and promoting our well-being.

Nutritional Tip 7
A Handful of Raisins

Raisins are an energizer and particularly beneficial for people trying to quit smoking. They are very rich in iron and also contain calcium, magnesium, phosphorus, potassium, copper, plus B1 and B6 vitamins. To restore depleted energy, eat a handful at 4:00 PM.

*Meditation is the power
in the individual
to take you through all adversities.*

— Yogi Bhajan

Meditation 8
Meditation to Reverse Any Negative Attitude, Frustration or Depression

PART I

- Sit with spine straight in a chair or cross-legged. Palms face each other at heart level, 12 inches apart.

- Move hands towards each other with each inhalation; away from each other with each exhalation. The arms swing wide to open the armpits. Keep fingers tense at all times.

- Move arms vigorously 7 times without the palms touching on the inhale. Count "one" through "seven." On the 8th count, powerfully clap the hands together in front of the heart center. Move at your own pace.

- Create a sweat.

Practice for 3 minutes.

- Relax for 3 minutes.

Meditation 8
Meditation to Reverse Any Negative Attitude, Frustration or Depression

PART 2

- Sit with spine straight in a chair or cross-legged. Touch thumbs and pinky fingers together.

- Move hands in a forward circular motion rolling over each other with the palms downward at the level of the heart center. Move rapidly. Breathe normally. You may find that the breath adjusts itself with the motion.

Practice for 3 minutes.

- To end, inhale and hold the breath for a few seconds. Then exhale and relax.

This two-part meditation immediately and spontaneously changes unwanted feelings and emotions to a positive and healthy state of mind. It reverses any negative attitude, frustration or depression. It also helps break habitual patterns.

Nutritional Tip 8
Garlic, Onions, Ginger — The Trinity Roots!

Eat garlic, onions and ginger for increased energy and sustained health.

Cooking tip: sauté one onion, about an inch of fresh ginger root and two cloves of garlic in a small amount of oil or ghee* until the onion is soft. Then add your favorite vegetables and spices. Continue cooking until the vegetables are tender. Delicious!

If you can't see God in all,
you can't see God at all.

– Yogi Bhajan

Meditation 9
Forgiveness Meditation (to focus on one or more people)

PART I

- Sit with spine straight in a chair or cross-legged. Rest hands on the knees. Repeat in silence:
  "I forgive everyone for everything they have ever done to harm me."

Practice for 3 minutes.

- To end, inhale and hold breath for a few seconds. Exhale and relax.

By extending forgiveness to another, anger and resentment are released.

PART 2

- Remain in the same posture. Mentally repeat:
  "I ask for and receive forgiveness for everything I have ever done to harm others."

Practice for 3 minutes.

- To end, inhale and hold breath for a few seconds. Exhale and relax.

By asking for and receiving forgiveness, guilt and shame are dissolved.

PART 3

- Lie on back. Mentally repeat:
  "I forgive myself; I dwell in love and light; I dwell in God."

Practice for 5 minutes.

- To end, inhale and hold breath for a few seconds. Exhale and relax.

The power of forgiveness transcends time and space and allows us to move forward with ease and confidence. As we forgive ourselves, forgive others and receive forgiveness, our hearts open to the light and love within.

Nutritional Tip 9
"P" Fruits

The "P" fruits, including pineapples, pears, peaches and plums, are all very good for the urinary tract, bladder, and kidneys. Incorporate any fruit that begins with the letter "p" into your diet and enjoy!

Every beat of your heart
is the rhythm of your soul.
The voice of your soul
is your breath.

— Yogi Bhajan

Breathing Technique 10
Breath of Fire

- Sit with spine straight in a chair or cross-legged. Hands are either in your lap or you may start with one hand resting lightly over the navel and the other hand resting on your knee.

- To begin, pant like a dog with the mouth slightly open, keeping your tongue in your mouth. On the inhalation, the navel will automatically push out and on the exhalation, the navel will automatically be pulled in. The focus of the energy is at the navel point. *On imagine I have dirt in my nose that I want to inhale out.*

My Solar Plexus, the seat of my personal power

- When you feel comfortable, close your mouth and bring both hands to rest on the knees, as you continue to breath powerfully and rapidly through the nose. The navel will automatically pump in and out. The inhalation and exhalation are equal in strength and length.

- Relax the face muscles *chest, rib cage & shoulders* as you continue the Breath of Fire.

Practice for 3 - 11 minutes a day. Enjoy!

- To end, inhale deeply and hold the breath in as you energize your entire body. *as mentally watch the energy circulate throughout my body.* Exhale and relax.

This is one of the most powerful breaths in Kundalini Yoga. It releases toxins built up by substance use from the body. It expands lung capacity and strengthens the nervous system which has been broken down through substance use. It also reduces addictive impulses for drugs, smoking and other compulsive behaviors. *A good tonic when my energy weakens.*

Nutritional Tip 10
Almonds

The almond contains many of the nutrients for strengthening the nervous system, including the B complex vitamins, copper, iron, phosphorus, calcium and potassium. They are best prepared as follows: Soak 6 to 8 almonds overnight in water, and in the morning simply peel off the skins. Enjoy!

We must not believe,
we must experience
that God is with us all the time.

– Yogi Bhajan

Meditation 11
Cross Heart Kirtan* Kriya*

- Sit with spine straight in a chair or cross-legged. Cross forearms below the wrist and hold them in front of the chest with the arms out slightly. Palms are face up and slightly turned toward the chest. To start, the thumb and second finger tips of each hand are touching with the rest of the fingers extended straight. Look at the tip of the nose and recite the following mantra* aloud:

  "SA TA NA MA"* (The "a's" are pronounced like "a" in "father.")

- As you recite each syllable, touch the thumbs to each fingertip, starting with the index finger:

  SA   index finger
  TA   middle finger
  NA   ring finger
  MA   little finger

- Continue repeating this sequence, always starting with the index finger. The pace between each movement is approximately 1 second per fingertip.

Practice for 11 - 31 minutes.

- To end, inhale, hold the breath for a few seconds, focus the eyes upward, exhale and relax.

  The words SA TA NA MA are the component parts of the mantra "Sat Nam," which means Truth is my identity.

  This meditation stimulates the nerve endings in the fingertips, balancing the right and the left hemispheres of the brain. This positively changes your habits and works through insecurities.

  Get ready...your spiritual unfoldment is about to shift into high gear!

60

Nutritional Tip 11
Sautéed Almonds for Women

Great during the female menses cycle and also the first forty days after giving birth. Sautéed almonds are a highly energizing treat. Heat a small amount of almond oil, butter or ghee* over medium flame. Add 6 to 8 whole *unpeeled* almonds and stir continuously until they begin to pop. Remove from heat and add honey to taste.

Kindness knows no defeat.
Caring has no end.
Touching a person's heart
is the only language God knows.

— Yogi Bhajan

Meditation 12
Meditation for Habituation

- Sit with spine straight in a chair or cross-legged.

- Make hands into fists, pressing the thumbs on the indentations of the temples.

- Lock the back molars together with closed mouth.

- Focus the eyes between the eyebrows.

- Breath normally with a relaxed breath.

- Silently repeat: **"SA, TA, NA, MA."** On each sound (approximately every second), vibrate the jaw muscles by pressing molars together and releasing. As you press them together, you will feel a movement at your temples.

Practice for 5 - 7 minutes. Gradually increase to 20 and then 31 minutes.

- To end, inhale and hold the breath for a few seconds. Exhale and relax.

The pressure of the thumbs on the temples triggers a reflex in the brain, activating the pineal gland. This corrects an imbalance related to the persistence of addiction.

This is one of the best meditations to specifically promote rehabilitation from drug dependence.

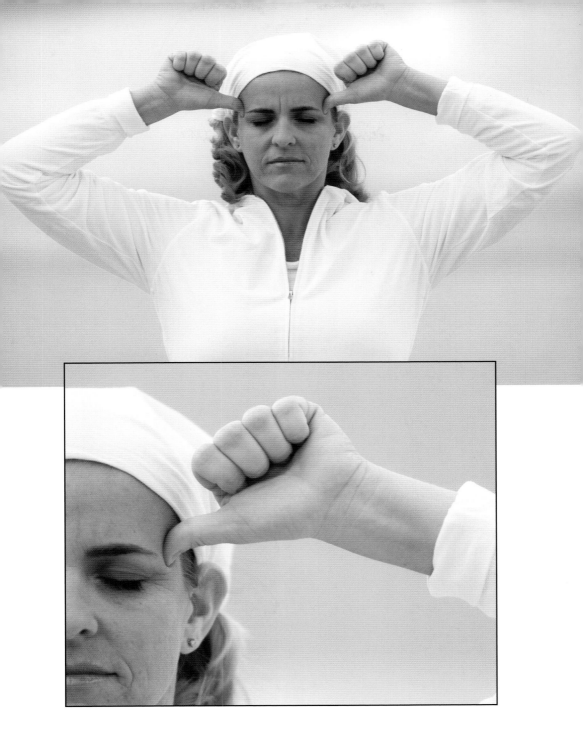

Nutritional Tip 12
Date Milk and Golden Milk

Date Milk
For a real energizer, all you need is 6 dates and 8 ounces of milk. Slice the dates in half and remove the pits. Simmer them in milk, on very low heat, for 20 minutes. Strain and serve.

Golden Milk
If you experience stiffness in your joints, this delicious drink is for you. It brings flexibility to the joints and will make you feel rejuvenated and youthful.

Turmeric* is a bright orange spice that can be found in a grocery store or health food store. It is excellent for joint lubrication.

1/4 tsp. turmeric
1/4 cup water
8 oz. milk
2 tbsp. raw almond oil
Honey to taste

Boil the turmeric in water for 8 minutes until it forms a thick paste. Add milk and bring to a boil. As soon as it boils, remove from heat and add almond oil. Serve with honey to taste.

Three Laws of Prosperity:
    Be kind to everyone
    Never speak ill of anyone
    Never speak ill of yourself
                    — Yogi Bhajan

Create a Positive Habit

- To achieve the best results, practice each meditation for 40 days.

- This is the amount of time required to create a new habit or break an addiction.

- The morning is the most favorable time to meditate. However, meditation is beneficial at anytime.

Service gives you everlasting friendship!

Crisis as a Blessing

Times of crisis can be the most opportune times to make profound and meaningful changes. Within each crisis is hidden potential and an opportunity to turn hardship into a blessing.

Learning from crisis and taking responsibility creates a shift in our thinking. Whenever we perceive a crisis as an opportunity, we achieve a victory in life. Every victory develops inner strength that allows us to face life without fear or guilt and to create a life full of peace, happiness and commitment.

Prayer

*It is our blessing to share these practices
for daily living with you,
to give a most precious experience,
and to enrich the quality of your life.*

*It is the birthright of all people to be happy
and to live in peace.*

This is our prayer.

Glossary

3HO - 3HO is the acronym for the Healthy, Happy, Holy Organization. See below for the definition of "Holy."

Aquarian Age - Beginning in 2012 this age will witness radical changes in consciousness and human sensitivity, and will embody the universal belief that God dwells within all.

Easy Pose - Sitting cross legged with the spine and neck straight and the shoulders and arms relaxed.

Ghee - Clarified butter; unsalted butter that is simmered down to remove moisture and allow the milk solids to separate and be discarded. Ghee is healthier than butter.

Heart Center - Located at the midline of the sternum, it is one of the energy centers in the body relating to compassion and love.

Holy - Refers to whole; the balance of one's physical, mental and spiritual being.

Humanology - A complete system of psychology to promote human excellence and spirit. It incorporates the technology of Kundalini Yoga and meditation and the principles of spiritual counseling.

Kirtan - Traditional devotional singing.

Kriya - Literally means a "completed action." In Kundalini Yoga it is a practice with particular effects on the body, psyche or self.

Kundalini Yoga - Known as the "yoga of awareness". Its practice rebuilds and strengthens many systems (nervous, glandular, etc.) directly affected by substance abuse and other behavioral addictions. Through the technology, the addictive personality is given the immunity to protect itself from the pressures of society. It is also perfect for people who want a relaxed and uplifting experience.

Mantra - Combination of words or syllables that help focus the mind. Practiced silently or aloud.

Navel Point - "Chi" energy. When this point is activated, there is a greater control over your energy. The end result is increased discipline and self containment protecting one from the temptations of addictive behavior taking over your life. Many meditations focus at the navel point.

Neck Lock - Gently move the chin towards the back of the neck, keeping the muscles of the neck, throat and face relaxed.

Ong Namo Guru Dev Namo - Ancient sounds to bring you to your inner wisdom. It is advised to chant this mantra 3-5 times before any Kundalini Yoga practice.

Sit with the spine straight in a chair or cross-legged with the hands together at the heart center in prayer pose. Take a long, deep breath and repeat **"Ong Namo Guru Dev Namo"** in one breath. If you need to, sip a little extra breath after "Ong Namo."

> Pronunciation:
> Ong: sounds like "song"
> Namo: sounds like the "a" in the word "ma" and the "o" in the word "go"
> Guru: sounds like "goo roo"
> Dev: sounds like the name "Dave"

Prayer Pose - Palms are together and upright at the heart. Right hand is the positive polarity and left hand the negative. This has a calming, neutralizing effect on the body and helps to focus the mind.

Sit in a chair - If it's uncomfortable to sit on the floor, it is just as beneficial to sit in a chair. Keep your spine straight and your weight balanced equally on both feet.

SA TA NA MA - Breakdown of words (mantra) Sat Nam which means "Truth is my Identity." See Meditation 11 for pronunciation.

Tip of the Nose - The eyelids relax so that both eyes are about 1/10th open and look towards the tip of the nose. This focus stimulates the pineal gland and the frontal lobe of the brain and helps to develop intuition.

Turmeric - Excellent spice for joint lubrication. Turmeric can be found in a grocery or health food store.

Sources

THE MEDITATIONS AND BREATHING TECHNIQUES

1 – Sadhana Guidelines, 1st Ed. P. 35.

2 – Guru Terath Kaur, *Dying Into Life.* (Guru Ram Das Books, 2006) p. 35.

3 – Sadhana Guidelines, 1st Ed. P. 68.

4 – Harbhajan Singh Khalsa, *Physical Wisdom.* (Ancient Healing Ways, 1994) p. 49.

5 – *The Aquarian Teacher, KRI, International Kundalini Yoga Teacher Training, Level One, Yoga Manual.* (Espanola, NM: Kundalini Research Institute, 2003) p. 397.

6 – Atma Singh Khalsa and Guruprem Kaur Khalsa, *A Year With the Master.* (Audio CD, 2001) p. 48.

7 – Yogi Bhajan and Gurucharan Singh Khalsa, *The Mind: Its Properties and Multiple Facets.* (KRI, 1998) p. 153.

8 – The instructions for this meditation are from the contemporaneous notes of Mukta Kaur Khalsa and could not be verified by KRI review.

9 – The instructions for this meditation are from the contemporaneous notes of Gurumeet Kaur Khalsa and could not be verified by KRI review.

10 – LA474, September 24, 1985.

11 – *The Mind: Its Properties and Multiple Facets.* P. 161.

12 – Sadhana Guidelines, 1st Ed. P. 11

NUTRITIONAL TIPS

1 – Alice Clagett, comp. *Yoga for Health and Healing.* (A.B. Clagett, 1995) p. 55.

2 – Amir Arberman, DC, ed. and comp. *The Ancient Art of Self Healing.* (Eugene, OR: Arbor Press, 1982) p. 65.

3 – This recipe is from the contemporaneous notes of Mukta Kaur Khalsa and could not be verified by KRI review.

4 – *The Ancient Art of Self Healing,* p. 90

5 – Gurubanda Singh Khalsa and Parmata Singh Khalsa, eds. Siri Amir Singh Khalsa, DC, comp. *Foods for Health and Healing.* (Berkeley/Pomona: Spiritual Community/KRI, 1984) p. 30-31.

6 – *Foods for Health and Healing*, pp. 45, 128.

7 – *Foods for Health and Healing*, pp. 52, 90.

8 – *Foods for Health and Healing*, p. 42.

9 – *Foods for Health and Healing*, p. 50-51

10 – *Foods for Health and Healing*, p. 29-30.

11 – Tarn Taran Kaur Khalsa. *The Gift of Giving Life, Vol. 2* (1983) p. 205.

12 – *Foods for Health and Healing*, p. 108

QUOTES

Page 13 – February 21, 1978

Page 21 – Aquarian Wisdom Calendar, January 28, 2004.

Page 25 – Aquarian Wisdom Calendar, June 16, 2007.

Page 29 – Aquarian Wisdom Calendar, October 21, 2003.

Page 33 – Aquarian Wisdom Calendar, December 29, 2005.

Page 37 – This quotation is from the contemporaneous notes of Nirinjan Kaur and could not be verified by KRI review.

Page 41 – From *Patience Pays* CD.

Page 45 – Aquarian Wisdom Calendar, November 4, 2003.

Page 51 – Aquarian Wisdom Calendar, September 23, 2004.

Page 55 – Yogi Bhajan, "The Mind" lecture given October 14, 2002.

Page 59 – Aquarian Wisdom Calendar, December 22, 2003.

Page 63 – This quotation is from the contemporaneous notes of Nirinjan Kaur and could not be verified by KRI review

Page 67 – This quotation is from the contemporaneous notes of Mukta Kaur Khalsa and could not be verified by KRI review

Professional Enhancement

We offer Super Health seminars and training based on Kundalini Yoga and Meditation to healthcare professionals and other groups.

These practical yogic techniques can complement traditional treatment programs by:
- Revitalizing and renewing energy levels
- Offering tools for change and to avoid burn-out
- Supporting a healthy lifestyle to improve the quality of your life

For further information please visit **www.super-health.net.**

Acknowledgments

I wish to personally express my sincere and heartfelt gratitude for the support of each and every one. It has been a consolidated effort to produce this book. A very special thank you to CJ (Dharam) and Mike Bigelow without their contribution this book would never have been produced. For their dedicated service and invaluable skills, I thank Nirinjan Kaur, Siri Neel Kaur Khalsa, Kudrat Kaur Khalsa, Gurumeet Kaur Khalsa, Kendra Mack, and Todd Hollien. I also wish to thank Carl and Roberta Deutsch, Kiersten Johnson, Erica Rosenast, Gabriel Rivera, David Nagem, Valentine Lahey, Sean Harner, Garrett Cheves, David Wilson, Kholi Hicks, Pat Campi, Tommy Massamino, Larry Kennedy, Laura Machieraldo, Debbie Tos Clombo, Bobbie Mannix, Michael d'Addio, Joseph Beartot, Zoe Zanidakis, Jesse Shriver, Wes Bailey, Kevel Kaur Khalsa, Bhagwant Singh Khalsa, Goran Perkunic; our models, Pamela Davis, Elena Tchou Tchenko, Miguel Dos Santos Manuel, Greg Khole, Kristina Kostrzenwa, Erin McKeever, Victor Larivee, Cornelia Nemorofski, Genevieve Mack, Kristin Briscoe, Sat Sundri, Da Vinci; and for their assistance, Harijiwan Singh Khalsa, Tej Kaur Khalsa, and Nam Hari Kaur Khalsa

May our prayer be heard as one voice, one determination and one strength for the upliftment of humanity and the exaltation of the human spirit.

— Mukta Kaur Khalsa

Resources

SuperHealth information:
www.super-health.net

Kundalini Yoga courses and events worldwide:
3HO Foundation
www.3ho.org

Information on courses and teacher training, books and DVDs:
Kundalini Research Institute
www.kriteachings.org

Music for Yoga and Meditation, Kundalini Yoga books and much more:
Ancient Healing Ways
www.a-healing.com

Music for Yoga and Meditation and Kundalini Yoga books:
Spirit Voyage Music
www.spiritvoyage.com